WHAT PEOPLE ARE SAYING

Celebrating Catholic Rites and Rituals in Religion Class

"A treasure of a book, *Celebrating Catholic Rites and Rituals in Religion Class* presents the primary symbols and gestures of the Catholic church in a simple but liturgical format that will enhance the faith development of children. It is very user-friendly. Catechists and religion teachers will easily see how and when to use these celebrations. Without a doubt this is one of the best things I have seen that does concrete liturgical catechesis. Anyone involved in the initiation and faith formation of children should have a copy."

—Maureen A. Kelly, MA
Author and lecturer in Christian Initiation
Director of Product Management, Resources for Christian Living

"Many books belong on the catechist's shelf. This doesn't. It belongs right next to every catechist as she/he plans each and every session. All that we do with children is formative, especially in our prayer experiences. Rituals are deeply prayerful as well as a powerful form of catechesis. They mold us, challenge us, and make real the mysteries we celebrate, but can't always put into words. Fortunately, the Catholic tradition touches the heart and soul through rituals.

"This book builds upon some of the most beautiful rituals we celebrate today as a Catholic community and adapts them to various settings with children, youth, and families. The faithfulness to our Catholic heritage is compelling; the practicality of each ritual celebration is heightened because of the several suggestions for various uses with different ages, different circumstances, and various liturgical seasons. The intergenerational component (uniting children/youth with older children/youth, parish members, parents, grandparents, catechists, etc.) provides an experience of the unity of our church. This book is a gift to each of us who walk prayerfully with children and youth."

—Sr. Janet Schaeffler, OP
Associate Director of Office of Religious Education
Detroit, MI

Celebrating Catholic Rites and Rituals in Religion Class

Kathy Chateau and Paula Miller

TWENTY-THIRD PUBLICATIONS

Mystic, CT 06355

Twenty-Third Publications
185 Willow Street
P.O. Box 180
Mystic, CT 06355
(860) 536-2611
1-800-321-0411

ISBN 0-89622-939-4
Library of Congress Catalog Card Number 98-60917
Printed in the U.S.A.

Contents

Celebrating Catholic Rites and Rituals in Religion Class

Introduction

There isn't a teacher or parent around who hasn't heard a child lament, "Mass is boring!" Our wise answer often is: "You only get out of it what you put in." This pat answer also challenges us to ask ourselves: What do *we* put into preparing for liturgy? How have *we* helped to create a meaningful experience for those we teach? Can we open the hearts of these children so God's grace can enter during our rituals?

Many children do not attend Mass regularly. Silence, ritual, and prayer may not be part of their ordinary experience. Our job as catechists is not only to "teach" the faith, but to allow the children to express and celebrate their own unique faith through prayer. Rituals embedded in ordinary experiences help create the atmosphere for this to happen. Our Christian rites, gestures, and prayers are "caught" through our consistent, prayerful, and meaningful use of them.

The liturgical celebrations of the Rite of Christian Initiation of Adults (RCIA) unfold our basic ritual symbols as Christians: the gathering of the assembly, the signing with the cross, proclaiming the Word, laying on of hands, anointing with oil, immersing in water, and sharing of the eucharistic meal. These ritual signs are inherently powerful forms of catechesis leading to deeper understanding of and commitment to faith. The classroom, whether in a school or religious education program, forms a faith community. By sharing these liturgical experiences there, we provide an atmosphere that encourages prayer, celebrates ritual, and connects meaning to liturgy, all of which are part of initiating children more fully into the Christian community.

We prepare children for liturgy by feeding their natural readiness for ritual. For example, as they see the liturgical colors on their class prayer table and notice the same colors at church, they will (sometimes with prompting) ask why there is so much purple around. When they have used water to bless themselves in class and heard some of the water stories from Scripture, they will better understand the sprinkling rite when it is done at Mass. When "faith buddies" share the Lord's Prayer with each other, they will echo that sharing each time they pray the Lord's Prayer at liturgy. These are the kinds of connections we hope to encourage in this book.

We will be focusing on liturgical experiences as an integral part of the formation of children within our Catholic community. Liturgy is central in the life of adult Catholics. So, too, we should provide meaningful liturgical experiences for our children. Thus, this book offers simple ways that you can use ritual in your religion class. For example, by setting up a prayer table and using the colors of the liturgical season, you can help children visually flow with the rhythm of the liturgical year. Simple rites such as "calling by name" and "signing of the senses" give children an awareness of belonging and purpose. The presentations of the Creed and the Lord's Prayer provide children with basic foundations of our faith. The reflections on water, oil, and bread invite a deeper understanding of our sacramental symbols.

A Shared Journey

Always keep in mind that we are not alone in our faith journey. Godparents and sponsors accompany the candidates and catechumens in the RCIA. Children in formation also need peer or companion sponsor groups. These peers and companions can be older children who walk with the younger children at various times. For example, seventh graders can be "buddied" with first graders to present and share the Lord's Prayer. Confirmation candidates can be paired with eucharist candidates to reflect upon their shared experience of baptism through a water rite.

If the curricula of two different grades focus on the same topic, those grades could meet together for shared ritual. When parish leaders schedule programs, perhaps they can look for opportunities for children and adults to share their faith. The opening prayer of the parish council, for example, could be an opportunity for these members to present the Creed to a religious education class that is meeting on the same evening. Intergenerational settings and family groups can also be ideal ways to provide companion groups and a larger faith community. Parents, of course, should be invited to participate whenever possible.

Always settle the children into a mode of prayer before you share a ritual experience. Children should be away from their desks (the "study" mode) and gathered around a prayer table in a comfortable position. A prayer table can be any small table covered with a colored cloth (in the liturgical color of the season). A Bible may be displayed there and perhaps other symbols that will be a part of your prayer (cruet of oil, bowl of water, etc.).

Quiet music or a song sung by the children can set the tone for prayer. Thus, with each of the rituals in this book, we suggest appropriate hymns to use.* Children can be introduced to silence, too, starting with a few moments of silence and lengthening the time gradually. Using simple strategies to focus their attention, like closing their eyes and listening to the rhythm of their breathing, can help ease the transition from busyness to prayer.

Note that we have included a related Scripture passage with each of the ritual celebrations. This can be read by you, or it can be read by a child or even several children. Invite readers to practice beforehand, however, so that God's Word will be proclaimed with reverence and care. Note too that all spoken parts are in boldface type for ease of use.

In order to keep the rituals simple and to allow them to speak for themselves, we recommend that any preparatory discussion should precede the actual ritual celebration. For example, in preparation for a reflection on bread, you might ask the children to think about different kinds of bread during the week before the prayer. This allows them to make their own connections to the prayer experience without having to explain too much during it.

If you choose to share a reflection as part of a ritual, keep it short and relate it to what you have already talked about in class. Or, you may prefer to reflect on the action you are about to share. With each ritual service, we offer suggested reflection topics to guide you should you want to include a brief reflection.

Our hope and our challenge is that the rituals in this book will inspire you to think about even more ways to help those you teach to make connections between religion class and liturgy. Perhaps, after all, the lament about Mass being "boring" is simply a sign that our children are truly hungry for meaningful spiritual connections.

*Most of these hymns can be found in **Today's Missal** (available from Oregon Catholic Press, 1-800-LITURGY), or in the **Gather** or **Lead Me, Guide Me** hymnals (available from GIA Publications, 1-800-442-1358). Special thanks to Curtis J. Murawski for his selection of appropriate songs.

Chapter 1

Signing of the Senses with a Cross

From now on, I carry the marks of Jesus branded on my body.
—Galatians 6:17

When we are first brought into the Catholic community we are marked with the sign of our belief in the Father, Son, and Holy Spirit. In the Initiation Rites (RCIA paragraph 266, p. 161), this signing is expanded to include not just a marking on the forehead but a signing of all the senses. Each time we enter the church building we again mark ourselves with this sign. Marking our body in this manner represents our total response to the life and death of Jesus, from head to toe. Children need to be reminded of the significance of being "marked" as followers of Jesus, and this first ritual celebration serves that purpose.

Uses

- This ritual can be used for the beginning of the school year to mark children as a community of believers.

- It can be linked to the signing with ashes on Ash Wednesday and throughout the lenten season as children focus on the cross of salvation.

- Lectionary-based catechetical groups can use this ritual when sharing the gospel stories of the man born blind or the healing of the deaf mute.

- Following the scope and sequence of the major religion textbooks, this ritual corresponds with the first-grade focus on the sacrament of baptism. Some third-grade texts focus on the Creed; the Sign of the Cross is the simplest creedal statement. Fifth graders look in-depth at the Creed and the sacraments. As children prepare for reconciliation they remember the times when their senses were "blocked" to the call of Jesus. This ritual can be part of a rededication to signify their reopening. This signing of the cross ritual can anticipate the signing with oil during confirmation preparation.

• To link this ritual to other classroom activities, you might consider "signing" the children at the end of class, using only one of the senses at a time.

• This signing can also be celebrated with children who are being sent forth from the community in acts of service to others. Prior to going to work at a soup kitchen or to do yard work for the elderly, for example, service-group members can be signed, reminding them that they are the hands, lips, and feet of Jesus.

Preparation

The prayer table should be set with a crucifix. Prepare the children the week before by discussing what it means to be marked with a sign. For example, jeans are stamped with a designer label, cattle are branded, and motorcycle bikers sport a club tattoo. All of these are signs of belonging to a group or identification of an image.

Have the children gather around the prayer table when you are ready to begin the ritual. Let the children know that the "signing" will involve touch and ask their permission.

When you trace the Sign of the Cross on each child, do so in silence. The signing of each sense (as below) may be followed by an acclamation of praise, recited or sung, such as: "Glory and praise to you, Lord Jesus Christ!" (David Haas, *Music for Christian Initiation*, Vol. I) or some setting of the Memorial Acclamation, "Lord, By Your Cross'" or this refrain from the Children's Eucharistic Prayer: "Jesus has given his life for us."

Song Suggestions

"By This Sign," Randall De Bruyn

"Were You There," traditional

"We Are Climbing Jacob's Ladder," traditional

Introduction

The cross is a central sign of being a Christian. Today I will mark you with the cross to remind you of how much Jesus loves you and that he is always with you.

Reading: Matthew 19:13–15

Then little children were being brought to him in order that he might lay his hands on them and pray. The disciples spoke sternly to those who brought them; but Jesus said, "Let the little children come to me, and do no stop them; for it is to such as these that the kingdom of heaven belongs." And he blessed them and went on his way.

The Gospel of the Lord.

Children's response: **Praise to you, Lord Jesus Christ.**

I mark your ears with the sign of the cross: HEAR the words of Christ.

Silence (pause), then sung or spoken acclamation by the children.

I mark your eyes with the sign of the cross: SEE the works of Christ.

Silence (pause), then sung or spoken acclamation by the children.

I mark your lips with the sign of the cross: SPEAK as Christ would speak.

Silence (pause), then sung or spoken acclamation by the children.

I mark the sign of the cross over your heart: MAKE your heart the home of Christ.

Silence (pause), then sung or spoken acclamation by the children.

I mark your shoulders with the sign of the cross: BE STRONG with the strength of Christ.

Silence (pause), then sung or spoken acclamation by the children.

I mark your hands with the sign of the cross: TOUCH others with the gentleness of Christ.

Silence (pause), then sung or spoken acclamation by the children.

I mark your feet with the sign of the cross: WALK in the way of Christ.

Silence (pause), then sung or spoken acclamation by the children.

Christ Jesus, our Savior and Brother, we have received your blessing on each of our senses. May we use them well to give you praise and to serve others. Walk with us from this day forward. Amen.

(This ritual is adapted from Rite of Acceptance, RCIA #268)

Closing Prayer

You may want to invite the children to hold hands as they recite the Glory Be together.

Let us pray together in praise of God who is always with us:

Glory be to the Father,
and to the Son,
and to the Holy Spirit,
as it was in the beginning,
is now, and ever shall be,
world without end. Amen.

CHAPTER 2

Called by Name

The Lord said to Jeremiah: Before I formed you in the womb I knew you, and before you were born I consecrated you.
—Jeremiah 1:5

In the Rite of Baptism all parents are asked, "What name do you give your child?" The response is the introduction of this new member into the community. A name signifies the dignity and total worth of this unique individual who is called by this title by God and the community.

In biblical times, names were more than an identification, they often revealed something about a person. Concerning Mary's child, Joseph was told in a dream, "You will name him Jesus because he will save people from their sins." Similarly, in biblical times a name change indicated a transformation in the person. When Abram and Sarai were chosen to parent a great nation, God renamed them Abraham (ancestor of a multitude) and Sarah (which implies a change of status, a new beginning).

In the Rite of Acceptance, catechumens for the first time publicly declare their intention to join the church and the church accepts them as members. As part of the Rite of Acceptance, these catechumens are called by name and asked what they desire of the church.

In the confirmation rite, candidates again are asked their names. This time they may choose to select a new name or reaffirm their baptismal name.

As children begin a new school year or program, they are in effect being called by name to enter into a faith community of peers. Thus this rite can be used during the first sessions of a religious education program or school year to welcome and accept these young Christians in formation.

Uses

- In a school or religious education class a prayer table with a Bible and candle can help children focus on prayer as a special time to be in God's presence. A "calling by name" ritual can be used at the beginning of each year at every grade level, since children are called to join a faith community of peers each year. Their response in faith grows as they do in age and wisdom.

- In a family-based program, parents call forth their own children. Parents are asked to be part of the ritual through their statement of intention with their children. In our particular family program, the calling by name was followed by sharing stories with children about their baptism, why parents brought their children to the sacrament, details of the day, importance of the name, and other memories of that special event.

Preparation

Sometimes it is best to use ideas from "shared reflection" (below) before the ritual, especially with young children. After the reading, the presider can then just refer to the discussion or ask a simple reflection question as, "How do you feel when the prophet says that you are honored in God's eyes?"

This ritual can set the tone for prayer gatherings in the classroom. Prepare children to come to the prayer table or circle with reverence.

Song Suggestions

"Your Name Shall Be Called," Ray Repp

"By Name I Have Called You," Carey Landry

"Shelter Me, O God," Marty Haugen

"I Have Loved You," Michael Joncas

"Will You Come and Follow Me," John Bell

Introduction

Explain to the children that you will be calling each of them by name to your prayer table. Once there, they will form a circle around the table and remain quiet until all the names have been called. You may want to have the children write out their full name on an index card (first name and middle name), so you can call them in a more formal manner.

Begin the ritual by inviting one child to carry the Bible to the prayer table and another to carry an unlit candle. Then solemnly light the candle and say, "Jesus Christ, Light of the World, you are here with us and you call us to follow you." Then turn to the children and begin (one by one) calling them forward. For example:

Leader: John Michael, I call you forth to follow Jesus…

Child: Here I am, Lord Jesus.

Leader: Lucy Marie, I call you forth to follow Jesus…

Child: Here I am, Lord Jesus.

Reading: Isaiah 49:1, 3

Listen to me, O coastlands, pay attention, you peoples from far away! The Lord called me before I was born, while I was in my mother's womb God named me.

The Word of the Lord

***Children's response*: Thanks be to God.**

Alternate readings: Isaiah 45:1, 4–6 or Genesis 12:1–5

Shared Reflection

How do the words of this reading make you feel? How does it feel to know that God chooses you by your own name?

Ask the children if they know why their name was chosen. Names have special meaning. Names give us a sense of belonging. God loves us by name. We belong to God.

Closing Blessing

Loving God, you know each of us by name and you love us. We thank you for calling us by name to follow Jesus. May we continue to follow him closely and may we grow in wisdom and grace. Amen.

CHAPTER 3

Water Rite

Those who drink the water that I give them will never be thirsty.
The water that I will give will become in them
a spring of water gushing up to eternal life.
—John 4:14

Three major sacramental symbols of our faith are water, oil, and bread. These symbols provide rich stimulants for our senses: the cool feel of water, the warmth and smell of bread, the soothing fragrance of oil. Reflection on these symbols help us to understand and connect their deep significance to our lives. Symbols and ritual are better experienced than explained. So it is best to expose children to them first, and discuss their significance afterward. You might use questions like: "How did you feel during this experience? What did you see? What did you hear?" Our first task is to allow the symbols to speak for themselves.

In our eucharistic liturgy, the water rite can be used in place of the penitential rite to signify our willingness to turn from sin. The signing and sprinkling with water can also be adapted for use within a penitential service.

Uses

• This ritual could begin or be part of catechesis on baptism. Most curricula cover baptism in first, third, and fifth grade. First and fifth grades might come together for a session to share an activity, video, or discussion of baptism. This ritual could open such a session.

• It would also work well as part of a baptismal preparation program for parents and families. Perhaps families who are preparing for the baptism of a child could visit a class studying baptism.

- Lectionary-based programs could use this ritual on the Feast of the Baptism of Our Lord.

- The signing and sprinkling with water can also be used as part of a class penitential service.

Preparation

Materials needed are a large bowl (clear glass is best), paper cups, and a pitcher of water. Place the bowl on your prayer table. Option: to stress the concept that the group forms ONE faith community, children could each bring in a container of water from home. (Of course, provide extra containers for those who might forget.)

If used as a penitential rite, talk about their experience of water at a beach. If we build a sand castle or write in the sand near the edge, water levels our castles and clears away our writing. That clearing or cleansing effect of water is celebrated when we say "Lord, have mercy," or "I confess to Almighty God."

You might ask the class about the importance of water. What is their experience of it? Fun…scary…refreshing…cleansing? Save any discussion of baptism for after the ritual. Keep your reflection brief to allow the rite itself to speak to the children.

Song Suggestions

"Let the Water Flow," Joe Dailey

"We Shall Draw Water," Paul Inwood

"Peace Is Flowing Like a River," Carey Landry

"You Have Been Baptized in Christ," Carey Landry

"Wade in the Water," traditional

"Baptized in Water," traditional

Introduction

Give each child a small cup of water (or have them use the container of water from home.) Invite them one by one to pour the water slowly into the bowl as a song is being played.

After the last cup is poured, all remain standing in a circle around the bowl, and the teacher prays:

God, our loving Creator, you give us new life

day after day, and the signs of your presence are all around us. From the beginning, your Spirit breathed on the waters, and through the ages, water has been a sign of your saving love and care. We were baptized with water as a sign of cleansing and new life. Today, may we once again remember that you call us to be holy and may your gift of water be our sign of this. Amen.

Shared Reflection

Here you may want to describe some of the experiences of water mentioned in Scripture. Also point out to children that the waters of baptism form us into ONE community, as the water is ONE. We bring the graces of the whole community with us and to others.

Blessing

Invite children to dip their hands in the water and sign themselves with the cross. Or, as in a penitential rite or a renewal of baptismal promises, you can sprinkle them with the water using an evergreen branch. Conclude as below.

God's voice calls to us to be cleansed in the waters.
Jesus calls to us to remember the waters of our baptism.
The Holy Spirit calls to us to accept God's everlasting waters.
Let us heed God's call this day and always. Amen.

CHAPTER 4

Enrollment
of Names

I have called your name, you are mine.
—Isaiah 43:1

The significance of a name has meaning for our present time just as it did in biblical times. Children put their name on the page whenever they begin a paper for class. We often begin class by calling names out publicly (taking the roll). People sign their names on a contract as a sign that they agree to its terms.

Names are offered for enrollment as part of the Rite of Election (RCIA, # 277ff). The names or the signatures of the candidates for the sacraments of initiation are written on a piece of paper and presented to the bishop. These are the candidates for full initiation into the Catholic community through baptism, confirmation, and eucharist. But the names are also publicly announced at the Rite of Sending to the Cathedral (held in the parish). This ceremony marks the final stage of preparation for the sacraments of initiation. Therefore it is appropriate that it be celebrated at the onset of the intense preparation. It routinely occurs on the First Sunday of Lent in anticipation of the Easter Vigil sacraments.

The names of those enrolled for the sacraments of confirmation and eucharist may also be publicly presented to the local parish or school community. It is the children's reaffirmation of their intention and properly should take place in the midst of the assembly that they are entering. The enrollment of names can be prepared in a separate ceremony in the classroom or as part of a sacramental preparation meeting. Participants sign a piece of paper which can then be presented or read.

This is also a public declaration of the community to select (or "elect") these sacramental candidates for fuller membership in their ranks. What a wonderful way to welcome the children to the larger group.

Uses

- This ritual is suitable for those preparing for the sacraments of eucharist and confirmation. As noted, it could take place at a sacramental meeting, in the classroom, or during a parish liturgy. It should be scheduled at the onset of the candidates' intense preparation for reception of the sacrament.

- This could also be at the beginning of a school year, or as a transition at the end of the school year. It could take place in the midst of the adults who are preparing for the sacraments of initiation in the parish, making a valid connection of initiation of both adults and children.

- In a liturgical setting, as part of the initiation rites, it occurs within the celebration of the Mass after the homily.

Preparation

Prior to this celebration, the children should think about how they would answer the questions posed in the ritual. They might write their private responses in their journal or quietly think about their reply during silent time offered in the classroom.

The ritual may take place in the classroom around the prayer table or in any site free from desks and routine study activity. A parchment could be prepared on which the students will sign their names (alternatively, this could have already been inscribed with their names). Afterward it can be hung in a prominent position in the church, especially during the children's liturgies, in the classroom, or in a prominent position in the school building.

Song Suggestions

"Who Calls You by Name," and "We Are Called," David Haas

"I Have Loved You," Michael Joncas

Introduction

Today you are taking a step closer to becoming fully initiated into the Catholic church through the sacrament of eucharist (confirmation).

Reading: Isaiah 43:1–2, 4

This is what the Lord says. Do not fear, for I have redeemed you; I have called you by name, you are mine. When you pass through the waters, I will be with you; when you walk through fire you shall not be burned, and the flame shall not consume you. You are precious in my sight, and honored, and I love you.

The Word of the Lord.

Children's response: Thanks be to God.

You have asked to share more fully in the sacramental life of the church. Are you sincere in your desire for eucharist (confirmation)?

Children's response: We are.

Have you listened well to the Word of God?

Children's response: We have.

Have you tried to live as faithful followers of Christ?

Children's response: We have.

Do you take part in this community's life of prayer and service?

Children's response: We do.

The church welcomes you into a time of prepa-

ration for the sacrament of eucharist (confirmation). Now you must let the whole church know that you have heard Christ calling you and that you want to follow him. Therefore, I invite you now to offer your names for enrollment.

The children give their names, either remaining in place or going with their godparents or peer companions, to the celebrant. The actual inscription of the names may be carried out in various ways. The candidates may inscribe their names themselves or they may call out their names, which are inscribed by their godparents, parents, peer companions, or by the catechist/teacher who presents the candidates.

God is always faithful to us. On our part, we must try to know, love, and serve the Lord more and more with each passing day. Continue to rely upon your godparents, parents, companions, and teachers for the help you will need to be faithful to the way of Jesus.

Closing Blessing

With hands outstretched over the children (sponsors or companions may place their right hand on the candidate's shoulder), pray these words:

Lord God, you created us and you give us life.

Bless these children and care for them.

May they be joyful in the life that has been won for us by Christ our Lord.

Children's response: **Amen.**

(adapted from Rite of Election for Children, RCIA, paragraphs 283-288)

CHAPTER 5

Ephphetha Rite

"Ephphetha," that is, "Be opened." —Mark 7:34

The Ephphetha Rite symbolizes the opening of the ears and mouth of the follower of Christ that they may hear the Word of God and profess it. Words and images bombard children constantly. They hear TV ads and programs, music, movies, and the constant pulsating noise of video games. Sometimes, they are exposed to so many voices, it is hard to distinguish the Word of God amidst all the babble.

This rite provides the pause and the direction to open their ears and mouth because something important and of value is to come.

Uses

- This rite may be used at the beginning of the year to awaken the child to the Word of God, especially before a presentation of a book of Scripture readings or a special textbook.

- Begin a retreat day with an Ephphetha Rite so those participants may center on the need to receive the message that will be spoken.

- Before peer mediation or conciliation, start with this rite to emphasize to those involved the necessity to be ready to listen to each other and to the divine counseling of God's Spirit.

- It may be repeated as classes resume after a lengthy holiday break.

Preparation

The prayer table should hold a Bible or lectionary in a prominent position.

Song Suggestions

"I Hear the Voice of Jesus," traditional

"Shine On Me," traditional

"Jesus, Heal Us," David Haas

"Healer of Our Every Ill," Marty Haugen

Introduction

Let us quiet ourselves so that we can listen to God's word for us. Take a deep breath. Now hold it in. Let the air out very slowly while you still your bodies and quiet your hearts to listen.

(You can repeat this breathing exercise until the group is settled.)

Now, trace the sign of the cross on yourself with your thumb as we pray:

God be in my mind (sign the forehead),

God be on my lips (sign the lips),

and God be in my heart (sign the chest).

Reading: Mark 7:31–37

The people brought to Jesus a deaf man who also had trouble speaking, and they begged him to lay his hand on the man. Jesus took him aside in private, away from the crowd, and he put his fingers into the man's ears. Then he spat and touched the man's tongue. Then looking up to heaven, Jesus sighed and said to him, "Ephphetha," that is, "Be opened." And immediately the man's ears were opened, his tongue was released, and he spoke plainly. Then Jesus ordered them to tell no one; but the more he ordered them, the more they talked about it.

**They were astounded beyond measure, saying,
"He has done everything well; he even makes
the deaf to hear and the mute to speak."**

The Gospel of the Lord.

Children's response: **Praise to you, Lord Jesus Christ.**

**The Lord Jesus made the deaf hear and the
dumb speak. May he soon touch your ears to
receive his word, and your mouth to proclaim
your faith, to the praise and glory of God the
Father.**

Children's response: **Amen.**

The children stand, one by one, before the catechist, sponsor, peer companion. The presider touches the right and left ear and the closed lips of the child with the thumb, making a sign of the cross, and says the following:

**Ephphetha: that is, be opened. May you profess
the faith you hear, to the praise and glory of
God.**

Children's response: **Amen.**

(adapted from the Ephphetha Rite, RCIA, paragraph 199)

CHAPTER 6

Acceptance of the Creed

We have found the Messiah. John 1:41

Through baptism we have been given a creed, a foundation of belief. Just as a child comes to know what it means to belong to a certain family, we grow in our understanding of the Creed and begin to claim it for ourselves.

In this rite, children hear the Creed read by members of the faith community. It is an invitation to take on these beliefs in a deeper way, to affirm them as their own. The Creed is passed on to enlighten us about the tenets of our faith. Our beliefs are contained in this brief document. Great theology is summarized in these few words which we repeat Sunday after Sunday. It is important during our formation to take these phrases apart and delve into the meaning of our faith. The power of what we say we believe is obtained not by dissecting or defining but by living these words day by day. And so we state what we believe today and what we hope to believe as we grow into our faith.

Uses

- This ritual can be used with the third and fifth grades as they study the Apostles' Creed in class. Often this is the core of the third-grade religion curriculum and would be appropriate to use at the beginning of that particular school year.

- Lectionary-based programs can use this rite during the third week of Lent in connection with RCIA groups.

- Confirmation candidates examine the Creed in depth and can accept the document as they begin their study or as they near the celebration of the sacrament.

- The tenets of the Creed are passed on to children from their parents, the members of their school community, and from their worshiping community. Different folks, depending upon which groups might be available to the children, could formally read the Creed. For example, during a school Mass the older students, the teachers and staff, or the daily Mass attendees might present their beliefs. After school, perhaps the parish council or a parish committee that meets at or near the time that the children are gathered for class can be invited to participate in this simple ritual. A written copy of the Creed can be given to the children.

Preparation

Place a brick on the prayer table. Have the table free of all other items to highlight this focal point for the prayer.

Song Suggestions

"God Is Building a House," Carey Landry

"If You Believe and I Believe," arr. by John L. Bell

Introduction

Today you are going to hear the Creed. It is a very important list of the beliefs of not only the Catholic church, but also of many other Christian churches. Let us first hear what Jesus says about the beliefs of the church.

Reading: Matthew 16:13–18

Jesus asked his disciples, "Who do people say that the Son of Man is? "And they said, "Some say John the Baptist, but others Elijah, and still others Jeremiah or one of the prophets." He said to them, "But who do you say that I am?" Simon Peter answered, "You are the Messiah, the Son of the living God." And Jesus answered him, "Blessed are you, Simon son of Jonah! For flesh and blood has not revealed this to you, but my Father in heaven."

The Gospel of the Lord.

Children's response: **Praise to You, Lord, Jesus Christ.**

Shared Reflection

Use any or all of the statements below as a guide for your reflection.

> **What kind of foundation does a house need? (Sand, mud, rock, brick). You also need a foundation for reading, for math, and for many other facets of life.**

> **Jesus told Peter he was a rock. What does that mean? How can a person be like a rock?**

> **I can believe new clothes will make me beautiful or loved, but it's not lasting. I can believe a new toy or game will make me popular, or I'll never be bored! But if I believe in something important and lasting, my house (me!) will be built on rock.**

> **I believe in God, God our creator, our parent. A God who is so close to us; a God who claims us all as children, brothers and sisters to one another. I believe in Jesus who was born a baby, lived a life of caring, died, and is risen with us today. I believe in the Holy Spirit, God's Spirit with us as we pray, as we gather. I believe that when we die, we join our family (all!) the communion of saints. I believe that if I sin, God will forgive me, others can forgive me just as I forgive others.**

> **I believe in life…forever! Our Creed is the brick of our faith. Our Creed gives us something lasting to believe in.**

Acceptance

Say to children: **Listen very carefully to the words that will now be spoken to you.**

Say to those proclaiming the Creed: And you, believers of the Creed, speak out boldly as you affirm it before these students.

Those who are ready to accept the Creed, please stand.

> My children, listen carefully to the words of faith.
> Receive them with open and faithful hearts.

Teachers and staff or significant members of the community present the Creed by stating it aloud line by line (the Nicene Creed or Apostles' Creed).

> **We believe in God…**

Blessing over each other

(extend hands over each other)

> Let us pray for one another, that we will know God in our hearts and respond with loving actions.
>
> Hold all of us in your tender care, O God, as we grow in faith. We ask this through Jesus, our source of light, justice, and truth. Amen.

Closing prayer

> Let us pray. All powerful God, your love is everlasting. It does not shift with the breeze; it is not here today and gone tomorrow. You are our God for all time. We are your children now and forever. O God, may we always be signs of your forgiveness and caring. We ask this through Jesus Christ, your Son and our brother, one God forever and ever.

Children's response: Amen.

CHAPTER 7

Profession of the Creed

You are the Messiah, the Son of the living God.
—Matthew 16:16

T he Profession of the Creed is celebrated by the children who have accepted the Creed at an earlier ceremony. They have received this statement of faith formally from the community. Now after some time of study and consciously trying to live out its tenets, they verbally proclaim the Creed to the community as their own.

Uses

- At the end of the third or fifth grade, if the class accepted the Creed within a group, perhaps they could profess it for the same community.

- Confirmation candidates can profess their beliefs to their sponsors, families, or other members of the community.

Preparation

Place a decorated copy of the Creed on the prayer table. If the theme of building a foundation was used during the presentation, you could again place a brick on the table.

Song Suggestions

"They'll Know We Are Christians," Peter Scholtes

"We Walk by Faith," Marty Haugen

"Without Seeing You," David Haas

Introduction

You have studied the Creed in your class. Now, your understanding has grown in the beliefs of our church. Since you have accepted these beliefs as your own, we ask you to listen carefully to the words of St. John. In this reading he describes some disciples who were having a difficult time with their belief in Jesus.

Reading: John 6:35, 60–71

Jesus said to them, "I am the bread of life. Whoever comes to me will never be hungry, and whoever believes in me will never be thirsty."

When many of his disciples heard it, they said, "This teaching is difficult; who can accept it?" But Jesus, aware that his disciples were complaining about it, said to them, "Does this offend you? Then what if you were to see the Son of Man ascending to where he was before? It is the spirit that gives life; the flesh is useless. The words that I have spoken to you are spirit and life. But among you there are some who do not believe." For Jesus knew from the first who were the ones that did not believe, and who was the one that would betray him. And he said, "For this reason I have told you that no one can come to me unless it is granted by the Father."

Because of this many of his disciples turned back and no longer went about with him. So Jesus asked the twelve, "Do you also wish to go away?" Simon Peter answered him, "Lord, to whom can we go? You have the words of eternal life. We have come to believe and know that you are the Holy One of God."

The Gospel of the Lord.

Children's response: **Praise to you, Lord Jesus Christ.**

The children now recite what was presented to them earlier in the year, either the Apostles' Creed or the Nicene Creed.

I believe in God...

Closing Prayer

Lord, we pray to you for these your children who have now accepted for themselves the loving purpose and the mysteries that you revealed in the life of your Son.

As they profess their belief with their lips, may they have faith in their hearts and accomplish your will in their lives.

We ask this through Christ our Lord. Amen.

(adapted from the Recitation of the Creed, RCIA, paragraph 195)

CHAPTER 8

Proclamation of the Our Father

Lord, teach us to pray.
—Luke 11:1

The Lord's Prayer expresses our primal relationship to God: as Abba, as Father, as Mother, as Family. The words echo God's indwelling and our connection to each other as brothers and sisters. It is our prayer for reconciliation, for breaking bread, and for sharing our lives.

The Lord's Prayer is the prayer of the church, an integral part of our daily prayer and liturgy. We proclaim the Lord's Prayer to candidates during the process of initiation. Our declaration to the children early in their initiation expresses the importance and prominence of this prayer in our Christian life.

Uses

- This ritual is ideal for proclaiming to first graders. Perhaps the younger students could be "buddied" with older students in the school or religious education program.

- Parents, grandparents, or other adult sponsors can proclaim this prayer to the children. If adults are not present, make sure a note is sent home with the copy of the prayer telling the parents about the presentation and inviting them to pray the Lord's Prayer with their children.

Preparation

Make copies of the Lord's Prayer (use a special typeface and heavy bond paper).

Song Suggestions

"Our Father, Our Mother," Joe Wise

"The Lord's Prayer," David Haas

"Our Father," Gregorian Chant

Introduction

Form a circle with sponsors behind the children to receive the prayer.

Reading: Luke 11:1–2, Matthew 6:9–13

[Jesus] was praying in a certain place, and after he had finished, one of his disciples said to him, "Lord, teach us to pray, as John taught his disciples." He said to them, "Pray then in this way:

Our Father in heaven, hallowed be your name. Your kingdom come. Your will be done on earth as it is in heaven. Give us this day our daily bread. And forgive us our debts, as we also have forgiven our debtors. And do not bring us to the time of trial, but rescue us from the evil one."

The Gospel of the Lord.

Children's response: **Praise to you, Lord Jesus Christ.**

Shared Reflection

What is prayer? Talk about how the children pray: asking, thanking, praising, praying together. Jesus teaches us to pray. Jesus was so close to God, he called God "Abba," a tender term for a mother, a father, a family member. When we pray, we don't have to say "Dear Sir" or "To Whom It May Concern." We call upon a Mom, a Dad, a Grandma, a Brother. If God is my parent and your parent, aren't we related?

Blessings

Sponsors (or big buddies, seventh graders, for example) lay hands on first graders; presider or teacher reads and children may echo each phrase:

> **Let us pray for these first graders, that they will always know God's love. May they always believe that God is in their hearts, and may they answer God through prayer and loving actions. We ask this through Jesus, our Lord. Amen.**

First graders raise hands over seventh graders; first-grade teacher reads and children may echo each phrase:

> **We pray for these seventh graders that they will always feel part of the loving family of God. May they be examples of God's care by their loving actions and prayer-filled lives. We ask this through Jesus, our Lord. Amen.**

Buddies give each other a copy of the Lord's Prayer that they have made or decorated, then say the prayer together in individual pairs. First and seventh graders can then share what this prayer means with their buddies.

Closing blessing

> **May we bring the love of this faith family to all our family members and everyone we meet. May God bless us and keep us close.**

Children's response: **Amen.**

CHAPTER 9

Presentation of a Bible

*Were not our hearts burning within us while he was talking to us
on the road, while he was opening the Scriptures to us?*
—Luke 24:32

The Bible is a story of God entering the lives of those who are open to the Word. The stories of Scripture are our stories. They are the basis of much of our Christian teaching and belief. The Bible is God's gift of revelation to us as well as his invitation for us to respond.

The Bible should always be read and presented with reverence while still maintaining a comfortableness to be "daily bread." Books containing the gospels may be presented to initiation candidates during the Rite of Acceptance. Candidates receive the gospels as a sign that they will share the Word of God with the Catholic community and learn to follow the instruction of Jesus.

Uses

• This rite may be adapted to present a religion textbook or another special book to students in the beginning of the year. This book to be presented contains special Bible stories and teachings which will help children to grow and respond in faith.

• Presenting the religion textbook to first graders.

• Giving the sixth-grade students a book of Hebrew Scriptures (the Old Testament).

- Those preparing for confirmation may receive a book of the gospels. Candidates for eucharist and reconciliation may receive a special sacramental preparation booklet.

- In the family program invite each household to bring in their family Bible. Parents could present the family Bible to their children.

- Children lectors, upon completing their training, may be presented with the lectionary.

Song Suggestions

"Take the Word of God with You," Christopher Walker

"Seed, Scattered and Sown," traditional

"God Has Made Us a Family," Carey Landry

"Speak, Lord," Gary Ault

Preparation

Have a procession. Carry the Bible with pageantry and enthrone it on a prayer table or other place of honor. With young children, the whole class can parade around the room.

Use incense or candles. Caution: if using incense you must prepare the children well in advance, for the pungent smell is often unfamiliar to them. Let them smell the unlit container of incense a day or two prior, and leave the opened box on your desk throughout the day so that the fragrance may drift about them. Explain that incense was used in ancient times during prayer. The Hebrew Scriptures talk about our prayers rising like incense to God. It is used today in our very important celebrations like the Easter Vigil, Easter Sunday, Christmas, and Holy Thursday. Remind children that a special incense, frankincense, was a gift of the kings to the baby Jesus.

It might be wise to test your classroom or other setting with burning incense before using it with the children in case it may set off the smoke alarms. Do not use store-bought incense cones, but arrange to get some real church incense. It is best when the children can make a connection with liturgy.

Introduction

Let us quiet ourselves so that we can listen to God's word for us. Take a deep breath. Now hold it in. Let the air out very slowly while you

still your bodies and quiet your hearts to listen. (Perhaps repeat this until the group is settled.) Trace the sign of the cross on yourself with your thumb as we pray:

God be in my mind (sign the forehead),

God be on my lips (sign the lips),

and God be in my heart (sign the chest).

Reading: Mark 4:1–20

Again [Jesus] began to teach in this way beside the sea. "Listen! A sower went out to sow and some seed fell on the path and the birds came and ate it up. Other seed fell on rocky ground, where there wasn't much soil, and it sprang up quickly, since it had no depth of soil. And when the sun rose it was scorched; and since it had no root, it withered away. Other seed fell among thorns, and the thorns grew up and choked it, and it yielded no grain. Other seed fell into good soil and brought forth grain, growing up and increasing and yielding thirty and sixty and a hundredfold." And Jesus said, "Let anyone with ears to hear listen!"

When he was alone, those who were around him along with the twelve asked him about the parable. And he said to them…"The sower sows the word. These are the ones on the path where the word is sown: when they hear, Satan immediately comes and takes away the word that is sown in them. And these are the ones sown on rocky ground: when they hear the word, the immediately receive it with joy. But they have no root, and endure only for a while; then, when trouble or persecution arises on account of the word, immediately they fall away. And others are those sown among the thorns; these are the ones who hear the word, but the cares of the world, and the lure of wealth, and the desire for other things come in and choke the word, and it yields nothing. And these are the ones sown on the good soil: they hear the word and accept it and bear fruit, thirty and sixty and a hundredfold."

The Gospel of the Lord.

Children's response: **Praise to you, Lord Jesus Christ.**

Shared Reflection

What did you hear in this story? When Jesus explains the parable, he says that the seed is the Word of God. What do you think the hard ground is? Who can the birds that eat the seeds be?

Just as the seed needs sunlight and water to nurture it, we need others to nurture our faith. Who helps us know God?

The Presentation

Presentation of Scripture:

"Receive the Word of God" or **"Receive the Gospel."**

Presentation of a textbook:

"Grow in the knowledge of Jesus." or similar words.

Children's response: "Amen" or "Thanks be to God."

Intercessions

That the Word become a seed planted in our heart, let us pray to the Lord.

Children's response: **Lord, hear our prayer.**

That the Word will grow and bear fruits of love and justice in our lives, let us pray to the Lord.

Children's response: **Lord, hear our prayer.**

That we may bring the Word to each other by our caring words and actions, let us pray to the Lord.

Children's response: Lord, hear our prayer.

That we will listen attentively and try to learn more about the words of the Bible, let us pray to the Lord.

Children's response: Lord, hear our prayer.

Closing Prayer

Loving God, you call us by name and speak to our hearts. You give us your holy Word to guide and strengthen us. In it, you speak to us about how to love all people, all our sisters and brothers all over the world. You tell us how to prepare for your kingdom and how to be your loving children.

Speak to us, O God, for we are listening.

We ask this through Christ our Lord.

Children's response: Amen.

CHAPTER 10

Presentation of a Cross

Lord, by your cross and resurrection, you have set us free.
(Traditional Prayer)

We sign ourselves almost absentmindedly so often during our prayers and liturgy that the Sign of the Cross has lost its meaning as a symbol of our faith. In order to restore some of the power of the signing, it is necessary to concentrate on this symbol in particular, apart from other marks of our faith.

Very young children can use body gesture to remind them of the cross. Stretching up, we open ourselves to touch God. Stretching across to each other, we reach to touch God by loving one another. Before prayer, the children could use these gestures to ready themselves.

Uses

- The Signing of the Cross might be used daily during Lent to mark and remember this special season. Teachers can sign the children with the cross as they leave religion class.

- In a family program, the children can also sign their parents with the cross. Families might bring their crosses from home for a blessing.

- Presentation of a cross can be used by first graders just learning their prayers.

Song Suggestions

"Take Up Your Cross," *Geistliche Lieder*

"If You Would Be My Disciples," Christopher Walker

"Lord, by Your Cross and Resurrection," (any setting of the Memorial Acclamation)

"Father, We Adore You," Terrye Coelho (sing as a round)

"Prayer for Peace," David Haas

Preparation

Place a crucifix on the prayer table.

As children enter the room, have music playing softly. Let them settle in comfortably for two or three full minutes of quiet.

Introduction

We come together as a class to focus on the cross of Jesus. So, let us stand and sign ourselves with the Sign of the Cross as we begin;

In the name of the Father...

(Thoughtfully make the Sign of the Cross. Use full body motions and repeat the signing twice.)

Let us pray,

O Lord, hear our prayer; answer us when we call.

Holy Spirit, lead us to a better understanding of the cross.

May our lives bear witness to the faith we profess, and our love bring others to the peace and joy of the gospel. We ask this though Christ our Lord.

Children's response: **Amen.**

Reading: Mark 8:31–36

Then [Jesus] began to teach them that the Son of Man must undergo great suffering, and be

rejected by the elders, the chief priests, and the scribes, and be killed, and after three days rise again. He said all this quite openly. And Peter took him aside and began to rebuke him. But turning and looking at his disciples, he rebuked Peter and said, "Get behind me, Satan! For you are setting your mind not on divine things but on human things."

He called the crowd with his disciples, and said to them, "If any of you want to become my followers, you must deny yourselves and take up your cross and follow me. Those who want to save their life will lose it, and those who lose their life for my sake, and for the sake of the gospel, will save it. For what will it profit them to gain the whole world and forfeit their life?"

The Gospel of the Lord.

Children's response: Praise to you, Lord Jesus Christ.

Shared Reflection

Explain to children that our outstretched bodies are shaped like a cross. Signing involves our whole self and includes both horizontal and vertical aspects. We are rooted in God and stretching out to one another.

Presentation

As you trace the sign of the cross on each forehead, say:

I mark you with the sign of the cross. It is the sign of Christians; let it always remind you how much God loves you.

As you make the presentation of the crosses, say:

You have been marked with the cross of Christ. Receive now the sign of his love.

As an option, children could have previously made simple crosses out of sticks and string. Instead of wearing the crosses, children can decide to put them in a special place to be a reminder of God's love.

Closing Prayer

This prayer of St. Patrick can be prayed as an echo prayer. Have children repeat each line after you and add gestures that they can imitate.

Christ be with me

Christ be beside me

Christ be before me

Christ be behind me

Christ be at my right hand

Christ be at my left hand

Christ be with me everywhere I go

Christ be my friend,

forever and ever Amen.

The following blessing should be prayed by the leader only:

And may God bless you this glorious day

The Father who holds the world together,

The Son who walked among us,

And the Spirit who makes each of us unique.

Children's response: **Amen.**

CHAPTER 11

Blessings

The Lord bless you and keep you.
—Numbers 6:24

A blessing is "a prayer that praises God and invokes God's blessing in the circumstances that have occasioned the rite" (*Catholic Household Blessings and Prayers*). Blessings are used to make us aware of God's presence in any situation, and they can be lavishly used. Biblically, blessings were only bestowed once. Once given, they could not be given again, as in Jacob receiving the blessing intended for his brother Esau. Blessings can and should be used in many situations. We commonly think of a blessing as we begin or leave a group setting, before we eat, as we begin a trip. Objects that we use in prayer can be blessed—an Advent wreath, a Christmas tree, candles, pictures. Special foods are blessed and used in celebrations, such as those eaten at Easter after the lenten fast.

In the classroom, children bless themselves at the beginning and end of prayer. Here we are concerned with a more overt blessing of the children by another—teacher, peer, parent, sponsor—to highlight the child's special relationship with God. Blessings are a sign of God's love and tender care. When they are bestowed, children can better understand that the church offers courage, joy, and peace as they proceed in their faith formation.

Uses

- Here is a simple daily blessing. As the children arrive for class (or leave), you can trace a cross on each forehead with the right thumb using a simple phrase, such as:

May God bless you and protect you this day. Amen.

- Blessings can be added to any prayer service and can be used to close a liturgy.

- Copies of special blessings could be sent home for family use at mealtime, during Advent, Lent, for birthdays, and many other occasions.

Blessings

As you offer the blessing, extend your hands in the direction of the children. Below are five possible blessings for class use.

Traditional Catholic blessing:

May almighty God bless you, the Father, the Son, and the Holy Spirit.

Children's response: **Amen.**

A blessing of Aaron (from Numbers 6:24–26):

May the Lord bless us and keep us.

Children's response: **Amen.**

Lord, make your face to shine upon us, and be gracious to us.

Children's response: **Amen.**

Lord, lift up your countenance upon us, and give us peace.

Children's response: **Amen.**

May almighty God bless us, the Father, the Son and the Holy Spirit.

Children's response: **Amen.**

A blessing of Paul (from Philippians 4:7):

> **May the peace of God, which surpasses all understanding, guard your hearts and your minds in Christ Jesus.**

Children's response: **Amen.**

> **May almighty God bless you, the Father, the Son and the Holy Spirit.**

Children's response: **Amen.**

A blessing in Ordinary Time:

> **Almighty God, keep us from all harm and bless us with every good gift.**

Children's response: **Amen.**

> **Set your word in our hearts and fill us with lasting joy.**

Children's response: **Amen.**

> **May we walk in your ways, always knowing what is right and good, until we enter our heavenly inheritance.**

Children's response: **Amen.**

> **May almighty God bless us, the Father, the Son and the Holy Spirit.**

Children's response: **Amen.**

A Blessing for Birthdays (from Catholic Household Blessings and Prayers):

> **Loving God,**
> **you created all the people of the world,**
> **and you know each of us by name.**

We thank you for (Name),
who celebrates his/her birthday.
Bless him/her with your love and friendship
that s/he may grow in wisdom,
knowledge, and grace.
May s/he love his/her family always
and be ever faithful to his/her friends.
We ask this through Christ our Lord.

Children's response: Amen.

May God, in whose presence our ancestors walked, bless you.

Children's response: Amen.

May God, who has been your shepherd from birth until now, keep you.

Children's response: Amen.

May God, who saves you from all harm, give you peace.

Children's response: Amen.

May almighty God bless you, the Father, the Son and the Holy Spirit.

Children's response: Amen.

CHAPTER 12

Affirmation by Godparents and Sponsors

I encourage you and testify that this is the true grace of God. Stand fast in it. —1 Peter 5:12

We are not alone on our faith journey. We need the support and nurturing of others. The early disciples wrote letters of affirmation to other communities. These letters encouraged, instructed, and sometimes disciplined the community.

Prior to the reception of the initiation sacraments, sponsors and godparents are asked to affirm candidates. They are asked to recommend the candidates to the church, giving testimony to their readiness.

Parents, grandparents, or even teachers can be asked to affirm and stand with children as they prepare for a sacrament. This affirmation ritual not only provides candidates with encouragement, but offers a supportive environment for the adult sponsor.

Uses

- Sacramental preparation meetings with parents and children.
- Classroom setting in a sacramental preparation year.

- When a child or small group is preparing for baptism or other sacrament within a setting where the majority have already been initiated.

Preparation

Testimony letters can be prepared for each sacramental candidate. Parents, grandparents, or other "sponsoring" adults can be asked to write a letter to the children affirming a gift of faith which they see in the child and offering encouragement and direction.

Song Suggestions

"Companions on the Journey," Carey Landry

"One Spirit, One Church," Kevin Keil, OCP

Introduction

Parents (sponsors, teachers), you are presenting these children for preparation for the reception of the sacrament of eucharist (confirmation). We are anxious to hear your words of support for them today. To prepare ourselves, let us listen to the words of St. Paul as he speaks out on behalf of the people he taught from the town of Philippi.

Reading: Philippians 1:1–11

Grace to you and peace from God our Father and the Lord Jesus Christ.

I thank my God every time I remember you, constantly praying with joy in every one of my prayers for all of you, because of your sharing in the gospel from the first day until now. I am confident of this, that the one who began a good work among you will bring it to completion by the day of Jesus Christ. It is right for me to think this way about all of you, because you hold me in your heart, for all of you share in

God's grace with me, both in my imprisonment and in the defense and confirmation of the gospel.

For God is my witness, how I long for all of you with the compassion of Christ Jesus. And this is my prayer, that your love may overflow more and more with knowledge and full insight to help you to determine what is best so that in the day of Christ you may be pure and blameless, having produced the harvest of righteousness that comes through Jesus Christ for the glory and praise of God.

The Word of the Lord.

All respond: **Thanks be to God.**

(Other optional readings from the greetings and farewells of the Letters: Romans 1:1–15 or 1 Corinthians 1:1–9.)

Shared Reflection

St. Paul wrote letters to his friends and to the communities where he preached to encourage, support, and help them grow in their understanding of Jesus Christ. Letters connect us. Isn't it great to receive a letter? Someone has taken the time to think about us. Like St. Paul, we have special letters to encourage your faith. Someone has taken the time to write to you, to tell you how important you are.

Letters are presented to the candidates. Allow a short time for sharing between adults and children.

Dear parents, godparents (grandparents, teachers) of this assembly: These children have asked to participate more fully in the sacramental life of the church. I invite you to give your recommendation on their behalf.

Allow time for each adult to freely speak about the child they are sponsoring or mentoring. They can respond to each question aloud to the entire group or they can tell the child personally.

Have these children shown sincere desire?

(Response)

Have they listened well to the word of God?

(Response)

Have they tried to live as followers of Jesus?

(Response)

Have they taken part of the community's life of service and prayer?

(Response)

Dear friends, you have spoken in favor of these children. Accept them as chosen sons and daughters in the Lord. Encourage them to live the way of the gospel. Offer them the support of your love and concern, and above all, be a good model to them of Christian living so that by your example they may grow deeper in the faith of the church.

All respond: **Amen.**

Blessing of the Children

Children, know that we are with you and will pray for you. May God bless and remain with you always: the Father, the Son and the Holy Spirit.

Children's response: **Amen.**

Go in peace to love and serve the Lord.

Children's response: **Thanks be to God.**

CHAPTER 13

Penitential Rite

*For I do not do the good I want but the evil I do not want
is what I do. —Romans 7:19*

We all sin. We make mistakes, make poor choices, and fall short of the goals we set for ourselves. The difference for Christians is that we know that we can ask for and receive forgiveness for our sins. We have occasions in our liturgies that are penitential. Also, the Rite of Penance offers us a celebration especially "to help children gradually form their conscience about sin in human life and about freedom from sin through Christ" (Rite of Penance, Form IV, paragraph 37). This penitential rite is similar to the scrutinies of the adult catechumens. It is a time to focus on forgiveness and to be strengthened by Jesus so we can better face our temptations. It is not sacramental absolution.

This gradual formation of a child's conscience can happen as a natural extension of their daily prayer. By taking a moment in prayer to help them focus on their behavior, we help them identify and name some personal faults.

Uses

- During regular class prayer time to ask for forgiveness of hurts caused during the day.

- Especially during the seasons of Advent and Lent to help focus on repentance.

- As an immediate preparation before receiving the sacrament of reconciliation, for all children as well as those receiving for the first time.

- As part of a retreat day prior to receiving confirmation.

- Make this rite a part of the fourth-grade study of the Ten Commandments and the Beatitudes.

Preparation

Find an examination of conscience in a children's current religious resource that is comfortable for you and your class. Dwell on one point during your prayer each class session. This reflection can be used daily or weekly to build toward the date of a sacramental celebration of penance.

Song Suggestion

Quiet instrumental music can be played during the examination of conscience.

Introduction

There are times that we have hurt others, or we have caused pain to ourselves, or we have broken the law of love that God sets out for us.

At this point, read one question from the examination of conscience. Allow a lengthy pause before using one of the optional penitential rites.

Because we are sorry for what we have done, let us take some time to ask God and our neighbors for forgiveness.

Different short penitential prayers from the sacramentary may be used such as:

Lord, Jesus, you raise us to new life.
Lord, have mercy.

Children's response: **Lord, have mercy.**

Christ Jesus, you bring light to those in darkness. Christ, have mercy.

Children's response: **Christ, have mercy.**

Lord Jesus, you feed us with your body and blood. Lord, have mercy.

Children's response: **Lord, have mercy.**

May almighty God have mercy on us, forgive us our sins and bring us to everlasting life. Amen.

Another option can be to say together the Confiteor from Mass:

I confess to Almighty God...

May almighty God have mercy on us, forgive us our sins and bring us to everlasting life. Amen.

Option three, the Lamb of God:

Lamb of God, you take away the sins of the world

Response: **Have mercy on us.**

Lamb of God, you take away the sins of the world

Response: **Have mercy on us.**

Lamb of God, you take away the sins of the world

Response: **Grant us peace.**

Option four, the Lord's Prayer:

Let us pray together the words of forgiveness that Jesus taught us,

> **Our Father...**

Closing Prayer

A good closing prayer may be a simple Sign of the Cross, a blessing, or sharing a sign of peace.

CHAPTER 14

Sign of Peace

Peace I leave with you; my peace I give to you.
—John 14:27

At liturgy, we take time to share peace before the Communion Rite. This outward sign acknowledges our desire to be reconciled with each other and the larger community. We know the command that before bringing our gift to the altar, we are to make peace with our brothers and sisters. In the spirit of that peacemaking and unity we observe this ritual for sharing some sign of peace among a community of children.

Uses

- There are often moments in class and program settings that call for an acknowledgment of peace. A shared sign of peace can provide a restoration of harmony.

- It can be used at the end of a class to invite the children to be bearers of peace to others they will encounter. This ritual may be used spontaneously, but the familiar and comfortable repetition provides security and leads to a understanding of the need for continual reconciliation in a community.

- Target one area. If a third-grade class is having a problem with hitting, talk about using hands (fists) to make peace and end the discussion with a sign of peace. A class dealing with harmful gossip might use this rite at the end their discussion about ways to use ears and mouths for peace.

- It may be used as part of a study of peacemakers, for example, Martin Luther King, Jr., Dorothy Day, or Mohandas Gandhi.

Preparation

The sign of peace can be a handshake or a kind, encouraging word such as, "I'm sorry" or "Let's do better" or "Great job!" The sign of peace can be a written promise or agreement to use peaceful means to end a playground argument, or to participate in conciliation. The sign of peace might reflect the area that is being targeted. For example, if hands are used inappropriately, a handshake or hug can turn those hurting hands into healing hands. Likewise for a hurtful mouth which now is used to say, "I'm sorry. Let's start over." Offending feet used for kicking or stomping in anger can be used to walk toward each other in peace.

Song Suggestions

"Peace Is Flowing Like a River," Carey Landry

"Prayer of St. Francis," Sebastian Temple

"Let There Be Peace on Earth," Sy Miller and Jill Jackson

Introduction

As a sign of turning away from hatred and hurting one another, our Lord Jesus gave us comforting words of peace. Listen to this prayer he spoke to his apostles. He says it now to us.

Reading: John 14:27

Peace I leave with you; my peace I give to you. I do not give to you as the world gives. Do not let your hearts be troubled, and do not let them be afraid.

The Gospel of the Lord.

Children's response: **Praise to you, Lord Jesus Christ.
The peace of the Lord be always with you.**

Children's response: **And also with you.**

Let us now share with one another a sign of peace.

Children take time to extend some offering of peace with one another.

Shared Reflection

To extend the theme of peace through reflection, you might discuss specific ways that the class can offer peace to others. Use these questions to guide you:

How do we use our hands to be peacemakers?

How do we use our mouths to be peacemakers?

How can we use our ears? Feet? Our whole selves?

Closing Prayer

Jesus, you left us the gift of your peace. May it fill our hearts and guide us toward offering your peace to everyone we meet. Jesus, Prince of Peace, pray for us that we might be true peacemakers.

Children's response: **Amen.**

CHAPTER 15

Laying On of Hands

I remind you to rekindle the gift of God that is within you through the laying on of my hands; for God did not give us a spirit of cowardice, but rather a spirit of power and of love of self-discipline.
—2 Timothy 1:6–7

L aying on of hands is a powerful gesture of prayer. Some of our most moving experiences of prayer with children have involved laying on of hands. During the presentation of the Lord's Prayer, when the little ones were to bless their big buddies, without prompting many of the big ones knelt down so that the little ones could reach them. In our family program, the first communion candidates knelt before their parents and the parents laid their hands on the children's heads and prayed for them.

We also see this gesture during confirmation, anointing of the sick, and ordination. In the RCIA, laying on of hands is used during the Scrutinies and Exorcisms. These are times when we call forth the Spirit, when we stir up the gifts of the Spirit within.

In the faith community of our classrooms, laying on of hands can be part of a penitential gesture during Advent or Lent. This rite is also associated with confirmation and can be used as a commissioning rite, a reminder of the Spirit, prompting us to act as we believe.

Uses

- As a part of the class discussion on social justice issues, for example, in the fourth-grade study of the corporal or spiritual works of mercy. Make a connection to a parish Christian service or community project where the children can get involved.

- When your class is facing a particular difficulty.

- This rite can also be used to commission a group before embarking on a service project or special event.

- The laying on of hands can be a sign of forgiveness when used in a penitential rite. Consider adding this gesture as a part of your closing prayer.

- Blessings (see chapter 11), combined with the laying on of hands impart a special sense of support. This can also be a powerful sign when the candidates receive this prayer as a part of their affirmation by their sponsor (see chapter 12).

Song Suggestions

"Lead Me, Guide Me," traditional

"Send Us Your Spirit," David Haas

"Peace Is Flowing like a River," Carey Landry

"Lay Your Hands," Carey Landry

Preparation

Laying on of hands is done in silence. No words are said, not even a prayer aloud. Do not have music playing. Allow the silence of the moment to speak. Although this may be strange or awkward at first, children, like all of us, need times of silence. Begin with just a minute or less and invite the children to be in touch with the God within themselves. Allow silence to be part of transition time. As you are more comfortable with silence, the children may grow more comfortable. Don't be discouraged, but keep trying to allow and invite moments of silence. Teach recollection by using phrases like "remember when…" or "imagine yourself…" or "take a moment to think about…" or "let's put away everything and just be in God's presence…" or "before we begin today, let's try to be totally quiet…" or "what happens when no one speaks?" or, "think about Jesus within you at this moment…." Add some breathing techniques: we inhale slowly the presence/power of God, then exhale slowly our own smallness/pettiness.

Introduction

Introduce this prayer with an understanding of what is expected, whether you are using the gestures in a sense of penance, or service, or blessing, or affirmation. See the appropriate chapters for possible introductory phrases.

Reading: John 20:19–23

Use this reading as a penitential rite.

> **When it was evening on that day, the first day of the week, and the doors of the house where the disciples had met were locked for fear of the Jews, Jesus came and stood among them and said, "Peace be with you." After he said this, he showed them his hands and his side. Then the disciples rejoiced when they saw the Lord. Jesus said to them again, "Peace be with you. As the Father has sent me, so I send you." When he had said this, he breathed on them and said to them, "Receive the Holy Spirit. If you forgive the sins of any, they are forgiven them; if you retain the sins of any, they are retained."**
>
> **The Gospel of the Lord.**

Children's response: **Praise to you, Lord Jesus Christ.**

Matthew 28:16–20

Use this reading as a commissioning rite:

> **Now the eleven disciples went to Galilee, to the mountain to which Jesus had directed them. When they saw him, they worshiped him; but some doubted. And Jesus came and said to them, "All authority in heaven and on earth has been given to me. Go therefore and make disciples of all nations, baptizing them in the name of the Father and of the Son and of the Holy Spirit, and teaching them to obey every-**

thing that I have commanded you. And remember, I am with you always, to the end of the age."

The Gospel of the Lord.

Children's response: **Praise to you, Lord Jesus Christ.**

Laying on of Hands

Teachers, catechists, sponsors, and parents may lay hands on the child's head. Hands are placed directly on the head and not held over the individual. The touch is prolonged while prayers are said in silence for the child.

Closing Prayer

Said with hands outstretched over the children

Let us pray.

Loving and forgiving God,

give these children

the Spirit of wisdom and understanding,

the spirit of right judgment and courage,

the spirit of knowledge and reverence.

Fill them with the spirit of wonder

and awe in your presence.

We ask this through Christ our Lord.

Children's response: **Amen.**

CHAPTER 16

Anointing
with Oil

The spirit of the Lord God is upon me,
because the Lord has anointed me. —Isaiah 61:1

Oil is a powerful biblical symbol. Oil lamps burned continually in the Jerusalem temple. Scented oil signaled festivity and brought welcome relief in a dry climate.

Oil graphically symbolizes the penetrating nature of the Holy Spirit. Oil is used in the sacrament of anointing to heal and enliven the sick. In baptism it is a sign of salvation and unity with Jesus conferring the identity of priest, prophet, and king. Confirmation bestows the seal of oil on the forehead that previously was washed in the baptismal waters. Oils connote something more permanent, or more lasting, more penetrating to the skin than the water.

Uses

- Anointing can be connected to signing or blessing an individual before embarking on a service project.

- During Advent the readings call us forth to be prophets. For the strength to carry out this ministry, an anointing can be used.

- During family prayer gatherings or retreat days, an anointing could be used as part of invocations for healing and strengthening the family. Parents' hands can be anointed as they are called to serve.

- As a part of preparation for confirmation, the candidates may be anointed with oil. Anoint their hands and not their heads. This allows the actual sacramental chrism to stand alone, rather than being confused or diluted with an anointing of the forehead prior to receiving this sacrament.
- Use this ritual as part of the fifth-grade survey of the seven sacraments and their major symbols.

Preparation

To help the children reflect upon the varied uses of oil, recall their experiences. Who has oiled a baseball glove? Why does a car need oil? If you close your eyes and try hard, can you almost smell McDonald's French fries? Have you rubbed lotion into dry hands or put Chapstick on cracked lips? Discuss the ability of oil to soften, smooth, nourish, heal, and illuminate.

Song Suggestions

"If You Believe and I Believe," John Bell

"He Has Anointed Me," Carey Landry

Introduction

Place a clear cruet of oil on the prayer table or in a prominent place. Have a small dish or bowl in which to pour the oil. You may want to use oil with a slight color and pleasant smell.

The Lord be with you.

Children's response: **And also with you.**

Today we pause to think about the symbol of oil. Let us call upon the Holy Spirit to help us be open to the healing, strengthening power of God.

Reading: 1 Samuel 16:1, 6–7, 10–13

The Lord said to Samuel, "How long will you grieve over Saul? I have rejected him from being king over Israel. Fill your horn with oil

and set out; I will send you to Jesse the Bethlehemite, for I have provided for myself a king among his sons."

When [Jesse and his sons] came, [Samuel] looked on Eliab and thought, "Surely the Lord's anointed is now before the Lord." But the Lord said to Samuel, "Do not look on his appearance or on the height of his stature, because I have rejected him; for the Lord does not see as mortals see; they look on the outward appearance, but the Lord looks on the heart."

Jesse made seven of his sons pass before Samuel, and Samuel said to Jesse, "The Lord has not chosen any of these." Samuel said to Jesse, "Are all your sons here?" And he said, "There remains yet the youngest, but he is keeping the sheep." And Samuel said to Jesse, "Send and bring him; for we will not sit down until he comes here." He sent and brought him in. Now he was ruddy, and had beautiful eyes, and was handsome. The Lord said, "Rise and anoint him; for this is the one." Then Samuel took the horn of oil, and anointed him in the presence of his brothers and the spirit of the Lord came mightily upon David from that day forward.

The Word of the Lord.

Children's response: Thanks be to God.

(optional reading Isaiah 61:1–2a.)

Prayer Over the Oil

God of all consolation, you chose and sent your Son to heal the world. Graciously listen to our prayer of faith. Send the power of the Holy Spirit, the Counselor, into this precious oil,

this fruit of the earth. Allow it to become your rich gift of healing and strength for your followers. We ask this through your Son, Jesus our Lord.

Children's response: **Amen.**

Anointing

Hold up the cruet of oil while singing or reciting "The Spirit of God rests upon me. The Spirit of God consecrates me. The Spirit of God bids me go forth to proclaim his peace, his joy." (Song melody by Lucien Deiss)

Pour the oil into small bowls for the catechists to anoint the children in their classes. They might sign the children or dip their own hands into the oil and rub it deeply into each child's skin. Music might be playing in the background during the signing. When all are finished, pause for silence then close.

Closing Prayer

Let us go forth to love and serve the Lord.

Children's response: **Thanks be to God.**

CHAPTER 17

Reflection on Bread

We have bread and wine. We need nothing more.
—Judges 19:19

"I am the Bread of Life," Jesus proclaims, By reflecting upon his words and this symbol, we can appreciate a fuller understanding of who Jesus is.

Bread is so ordinary that families all over the world offer some form of it on their tables every day. Bread is elevated from the ordinary to the sacred through the actions of Jesus. Bread serves as one of the central Christian symbols in the eucharist. The breaking of bread is so powerful an experience that Jesus is recognized in the sharing. Breaking bread today invites us into communion with one another.

In this reflection, the process of making bread relates how Jesus' life and our lives are mixed and formed by faith.

Uses

- During eucharist preparation both parents and children can reflect upon the symbol of bread—at a sacramental parent meeting or a family retreat day.

- Eucharist candidates can be "buddied" with older students in the Catholic school or religious education programs to enjoy this reflection.

- The fifth-grade students can share this reflection as part of their curriculum on the sacraments.

Preparation

The presenter needs to gather: apron, glass bowl, flour, water, yeast, salt, oil, spoon, wet towel. Also have a familiar recipe for your favorite bread, a shaft of wheat, bread in the process of rising (covered in a bowl), and a loaf of freshly baked bread. Prepare Scripture passages on cards for students to read.

If possible, have the class name as many forms of bread as they can: pita, whole wheat, French toast, bagels, etc.

Song Suggestions

"We Come to Your Table," Carey Landry

"Jesus, You are Bread for Us," Christopher Walker

"To Be Your Bread," David Haas

"Eat This Bread," Jacques Berthier

Introduction

There are many types of bread. (Use examples that the class came up with.) In the Bible, there are over 200 references to bread. Reflecting on bread can help us think about Jesus' life.

Prayer

Give eight students note cards with short readings and lines from Scripture that refer to bread. Pause briefly for silent prayer after each is read.

> **1. Exodus 16:4 Then the Lord said to Moses, "I am going to rain down bread from heaven for you, and each day the people shall go out and gather enough for that day."**

> **2. Judges 19:19 We have bread and wine. We need nothing more.**

> **3. Isaiah 55:2 Why do you spend your money for that which is not bread, and your labor for that which does not satisfy?**

4. Matthew 6:11–12 Give us this day our daily bread. And forgive us our debts as we also have forgiven our debtors.

5. John 6:35 I am the bread of life. Whoever comes to me will never be hungry.

6. Matthew 26:26 While they were eating, Jesus took a loaf of bread, and after blessing it he broke it, gave it to the disciples, and said, "Take, eat; this is my body."

7. Luke 24:30–31 When he was at table with them, he took bread, blessed and broke it, and gave it to them. Then their eyes were opened, and they recognized him.

8. 1 Corinthians 10:16–17 The bread that we break, is it not a sharing in the body of Christ? Because there is one bread, we who are many are one body, for we all partake of the one bread.

Shared Reflection

Making bread can help us think about Jesus. Reflect on this with participants while making the bread.

Hold up piece of wheat.

> **Unless a grain of wheat falls to the earth, it remains a grain of wheat. It needs soil, sun, and water to grow. We need others to grow.**

The wheat is crushed to make flour.

> **Jesus' life was crushed for our life. Sometimes we are able to do difficult things out of love.**

Add water.

Through baptism we receive the water of life, cleansing water.

Add yeast.

The Word of God is the yeast that grows in us.

A little oil.

Baptism, anointing, and confirmation are sacred moments when we experience the healing power of oil.

A little salt.

We are not to be bland people; we are the salt of the earth.

Kneading.

Bread takes time. The Word, the waters, the oil, need to be worked through our life. God gently pushes and pulls us. The hand of God works on us. Bread takes time.

Cover and let rise.

We need time for quiet, for reflection and prayer. We can't rush bread. It takes times to love, have faith, grow.

Bake.

The warmth of the community helps finish us; we need one another. Bread is meant to be shared. We are bread for others, and Jesus is the bread of life for all of us.

Blessing and commissioning

Break the freshly baked bread and pass it along saying:

From now on, let us be bread to one another.

CHAPTER 18

Celebrations of the Word of God

*For as the rain and the snow come down from heaven, and do not
return there until they have watered the earth, so shall my word be
that goes out from my mouth; it shall not return to me empty.*
—Isaiah 55:10–11

Formation into the church is in large part formation by the Word of
God. The celebration of the Word in the rhythm of the liturgical seasons implants central teachings, provides a rich source for reflection
and prayer, and prepares the children for fuller participation in liturgy.

The celebration of the Word can be used as part of classroom prayer or with
penitential or other prayer services. A meaningful presentation of the Word can
be woven into every class by always giving the Word special distinction.

Keep a classroom Bible in a prominent place. Process with it held high.
Always read from it with reverence to emphasize the importance of God's Word.

Uses

- Any time Scripture is read from the textbook, God's Word can be emphasized
  by standing, gathering around a prayer table, allowing silence, or using a
  song or response.

- No matter what textbook series is used, the teacher can set aside part or all
  of a religion class for celebration of the Word from the Sunday readings. The

lectionary is your guide.

- In religious education programs, the catechist needs to incorporate Scripture whenever possible.
- Begin parent and family meetings with a presentation of the Word.

Song suggestions

Music for Children's Liturgy of the Word, Christopher Walker

Refrain to "Praise to You, O Christ Our Savior," Bernadette Farrell

"God Has Made Us a Family," with verse 2, Carey Landry

"Sing God a Simple Song," Diana Kodner

Reading of the Word

Proclaim (don't just read) the Scripture passage for the day.

Use the familiar exchange of responses—

The Word of the Lord. Thanks be to God.

The Gospel of the Lord. Praise to You, Lord Jesus Christ.

Responsorial Psalm

Consider using gesture with your songs.

Shared Reflection

Ask children what they have heard. Listen carefully to what they say.

Reflect the children's words back to them and pull some of their thoughts together with one or two main ideas. Don't be discouraged that you may not be a Scripture scholar and might not have answers for every question. Let the Word speak to you. There are many resources for Liturgy of the Word that can help you share these reflections. (Examples: *Celebrating the Lectionary*, *Celebrating the Good News*, and *Sunday*.)

Closing Prayer and Blessing

Loving God, open our minds and hearts that we might believe in your holy Word and share

its message with everyone we meet. Guide us and give us the courage to do what is right.

Children's response: Amen.

Cross Reference Connections
with the Eucharistic Liturgy

Cross Reference
Connections by Grade

Resources

Rite of Christian Initiation of Adults, Liturgy Training Publications, Chicago: 1988.

The Christian Initiation of Children: Hope for the Future, Robert D. Duggan and Maureen A. Kelly, Paulist Press, New York: 1991.

The Rites of the Catholic Church, Volume One. The Liturgical Press, Collegeville, MN: 1990. Rite of Baptism, Rite of Confirmation, Rite of Penance.

Book of Blessings. The Liturgical Press, Collegeville, MN: 1989.

Catholic Household Blessings and Prayers, United States Catholic Conference, Inc., 1989.

Children's Daily Prayer, Elizabeth McMahon Jeep, Liturgy Training Publications, published annually.

The Sacramentary; Lectionary for Mass; Lectionary for Masses with Children; Directory of Masses with Children: Catholic Book Publishing Co., New York.

Celebrating the Lectionary, Elizabeth Montes, ed. Resource Publications, San Jose: published annually.

Celebrate the Good News. Maureen Kelly, Living the Good News, Inc. Denver, CO: published quarterly.

Sunday. Treehaus Communications, Inc. Loveland, Ohio: 1994.

Of Related Interest...

20 Prayer Lessons for Children

PHYLLIS VOS WEZEMAN AND JUDE DENNIS FOURNIER

Here is a fun and faith-filled guide to teaching prayer. Each simple and direct lesson centers around an activity designed to bring out a particular prayer theme. Activities include drama, dance, games, music, storytelling, and art.

ISBN: 0-89622-689-1, 64 pp, $9.95

20 More Prayer Lessons for Children

PHYLLIS VOS WEZEMAN AND JUDE DENNIS FOURNIER

Opens the door to creative techniques and straight-forward ideas, giving those who work with children the means to build lifelong prayer habits and patterns. Practical lessons center around an activity designed to bring out a particular prayer theme.

ISBN: 0-89622-689-1, 64 pp, $9.95

25 Guided Prayer Services for Middle Graders

PAT EGAN DEXTER

This creative, user-friendly prayer service book connects the real-life experiences of children with the words of Scripture. Each service highlights one of the many gifts children have received from God. Topics include the virtues: joy, love, friendship, trust, and forgiveness; physical gifts: hearts that love and hands that feel and touch; gifts of nature: water, fire, and rock; and spiritual gifts: God's law, suffering, and healing.

ISBN: 0-89622-688-3, 88 pp, $12.95

50 Children's Liturgies for All Occasions

FRANCESCA KELLY

A great resource for planning liturgies for children in grades K-3. Each contains an opening prayer, first reading, responsorial psalm, Gospel acclamation, Gospel, prayer of the faithful, preparation of gifts, communion prayer, closing prayer, and final blessing.

ISBN: 0-89622-541-0, 200 pp, $12.95

Children, Imagination, and Prayer
Creative Techniques for Middle Grade Students
PAT EGAN DEXTER

Using techniques that combine imagination, relaxation, and guided imagery, the author gives step-by-step directions for bringing students to a new and meditative experience of prayer, referred to as "picture prayer." Part One shows teachers how to help students understand why and how picture prayer works. Part Two offers ten step-by-step exercises on various themes which guide students into picture prayer. Great help for busy teachers and parents.

ISBN: 0-89622-565-8, 80 pp, $7.95

Acting Out the Miracles and Parables
52 Five-Minute Plays for Education and Worship
SR. MARY KATHLEEN GLAVICH

Here are 28 of the most memorable miracle stories and 24 favorite parables from the pages of the four gospels. Every playlet is adaptable for every grade and is sure to enliven and enrich religion classes and "do learning" in a way that students will remember. Includes a thematic index and worship reference guide.

ISBN: 0-89622-363-9, 144 pp, $12.95

Available at religious bookstores or from:

TWENTY-THIRD PUBLICATIONS
P.O. BOX 180 • MYSTIC, CT 06355
1-800-321-0411 • E-Mail:ttpubs@aol.com